Flying Horses

Flying Horses

poems

Jeanne Lohmann

2001 · FITHIAN PRESS, SANTA BARBARA, CALIFORNIA

Thanks to the editors and publishers of periodicals and collections in which these poems first appeared:

Abiko Quarterly: At the Cedar Gate
Atlanta Review: In Heavy Fall of Rain
Argestes: Narrow Boat, Long River
Barnabe Mountain Review: Three Cemeteries: a Meditation
Bellowing Ark: The Hawk; Tulips
The Bitter Oleander: In the Desert at Night
Blue Unicorn: Dogwood
Buffalo Spree: Anniversary; Claiming the Season
Calapooya Collage: Sea Song Out of *Beowulf*
Crab Creek Review: If Death Is a Woman
EarthLight: Calling the Barred Owl
Friends Bulletin: Listen, John Donne
High Country News: In the Open
The MacGuffin: Blackberry-Picking
Mickle Street Review: On Studying Whitman Indoors
Northwest Literary Forum: With Friends in Hanazono
Passages North: The Accident
Poetry Northwest: Flying Horses
Bulletin (Poetry Society of America): Picking Plums
Rain City Review: A Habit of Conversation; Peripheral Vision
The Raven Chronicles: January Moss; Northwest Woodcarver; The Seals
Santa Barbara Review: Visiting in Amherst: Two Poems
Santa Clara Review: Passing Through
Spillway: All the Way Out (forthcoming)
Shenandoah: Children in a Cemetery, Kyoto; The Headlands
Yankee: Whistle (forthcoming)

"October Moon, New England Church" was published in the anthology *Wild Song,* and "Eelgrass, Padilla Bay" in *The Padilla Bay Poets Anthology, 1995–1997.* Other poems are from two chapbooks, *Gathering Stones* and *Ends of the Earth* (New Market Press), and from out-of-print collections.

Published by Fithian Press
A division of Daniel and Daniel, Publishers, Inc.
Post Office Box 1525
Santa Barbara, CA 93102
www.danielpublishing.com

LIBRARY OF CONGRESS CATALOGING-IN-PUBLICATION DATA
Lohmann, Jeanne.
    Flying horses : poems / by Jeanne Lohmann.
      p.   cm.
    ISBN 1-56474-351-9
    I. Title.
PS3562.O463 F58 2001
811'.54—dc21   00-009949

Contents

In the journeys of the heart, be alert for the slightest sign. Along the extraordinary blue corridors of the soul, take nothing for granted.

One

Flying Horses

1.

In my early fantasies I thought if the day comes
I dare to climb on the Flying A red horse
on the gas station pole at the corner
of Fifth and Main, if the day ever comes
I take the golden bridle in hand and pass
through clouds and stars, the great wings
opening and closing as we flap through the universe
toward the Chimera that waits in the night
to vomit the lead from its jaws, would I
be bold to risk such transformation,
seize the bright mane though it burn my fingers,
though heaven's air is thin and hard to breathe,
though planets spin and die around us?

2.

In my late life, and hoping the muse would bless me,
in Firenze's Boboli Gardens I asked my love
to take a picture where I stood next to the statue,
Pegasus tamed by white marble. Born of the gorgon's
blood, there was no sign of the wound that bore him,
no light in the unmoving eyes. The merciless wings
did not close, no feather fell to the ground,
silence heavy in the body, the muscled flanks and back,
one perfect foreleg lifted and ready to rise. My head
hardly reached to the pedestal base, my hand
on stone struck no spark from a single hoof.

3.

Centaur, bareback rider, feet and legs bare
to the rough wet hide of horse, thighs and knees
fitting his ribcage, our two hearts pumping,
his long muscles expand, contract under skin
that rolls against me smooth as water.
Night rushes past, another dark rider
flying ahead of the sea-wind,
its bitter smell of dunegrass and kelp.
At Half Moon Bay the beach goes on forever.
Bent low to the hot and straining neck
my body staccato hoofbeats on hard sand,
the roar of invisible ocean
in our four ears
we are saltspray and foam
and the moon will never catch us.

One Summer in Rome

Sometimes we see the world as it happens,
acknowledge with our bare attention the singular presence
of days that come on us like gifts: like walking into
a spacious Roman house with cool polished floors
and geometric-patterned rugs, the Greek vases, the books
and paintings—art and history so perfectly in place
to welcome us after the frantic pace of the city,
the *statzione di treni*. Sometimes we see and frame
such moments, the plain facts
their own epiphany.

Years after, I remember my Latin teacher,
Miss Adams, her love for the "dead" language, remember
drawings and photographs on the shiny pages of the text,
descriptions of Rome, the arrangement of houses: atrium,
      columns,
the household gods Lares and Penates on the hearth, how matrons
dressed and wore their hair, citizens in their white togas,
the lectors carrying the fasces symbol of office, laurel wreaths
on the heads of Caesars, the decadent feasts.

Guests and latecomers to late summer
in this old garden, our feast *prosciutto e fichi* (in Italy
some magic happens with this combination, our host said),
and melon, *formaggio*, olives, long Italian tomatoes, wonderful
many-shaped breads, wine and *torrone*, strips of apricot and
fig leather. Sunlight filtered down through the graygreen
olive leaves and the arbor, the full clusters of the grapes
tight in their warm skins. Bees buzzed through the long afternoon.

Scrawny cats and their kittens
run wild in the arena, the honeycomb cells of the coliseum.
Tourists at Trevi toss coins from their car windows, ignore
the legendary water. Lost in the crowds at St. Peter's, I saw
a country priest with his round black hat held close to his chest,
his expression awed and bewildered as if like Saint Francis
in all this magnificence he was hunting for God. Sometimes
we see the world as it happens, a presence.

But I did not think then of my teacher
or recitations in school, words in a language I have forgotten,
stories and ruins, the conquering legions, and Christians
in the catacombs. They were present and with me, alive
and enduring as marble, the old aqueducts, the Baths of Caracalla,
lessons well-made as the Roman roads a traveler still uses.

Sidewalk Cafe

Late August in the evening light
Zurich found a mildness now
it was closing time. Theaters
were out, the traffic gone.
The waiters knew their work
was nearly done, and greeted us
with less than grace,
though expert charm stayed easy,
almost warm. This final night
we had no need of wine,
but weary and at ease
were quite content, and watched
how light reflected from the stone.

Tomorrow's flight would take us home.
We'd walked these foreign cobbled streets
the length of summer long, and here
our talk was full of all the day
had been, the presents we had found
and suitcase room for packing them,
our children we would see. Your hand
was on my own. Familiar quiet settled down.

Two women near us rose to leave,
and stopping by our table asked
if they might interrupt to tell
how seeing us they paused.
They came, they said, to praise
the ways we looked our love, some joy
we might not know shone through.
For this our language had no words.
We thanked these strangers for their gift,
and smiled. All that we knew
we could not ever say.

Across the Warp

Whatever comes, face into that. We can't know
what the tapestry will look like, finished.
This rough underside, this is where we work

against the threads' resistance, the tangled
colors. No machine equipped to take over
and complete the piece, only intense labor

persistent as the wish that we'll be allowed
to see it through (though something asks
why we should be so favored). Few works

make it to the exhibition. Still, if we examine
the texture, the warp and woof of what happens,
we could find patience in the small stitches,

recall the time required to make one square yard
of tapestries in Florence, the great walls
in the Galleria dell' Accademia:

Adam naming the animals, Eve offering the apple,
the tender details, how the bodies fit into space
and flow. And the curve where Adam's rib

was drawn out, no black outline, but rather
the suggestion of power entering and leaving,
a bright and formless opening.

Three Cemeteries: A Meditation

In California, a row of cypresses, spires more eloquent than steeples,
leads to the grave, a flat stone we have trouble finding.
Grass infringes the edges, artificial flowers relieve the living
of too frequent attention to the dead, for whom after all we're not
responsible. We come here to talk, to listen to their silence,
speech we have to hear, voices that won't be heard unless
we take the time. It is unequal conversation. The dead weigh more.

In countryside near Cremona we saw an old woman in black
go through an iron gate between walls of umber-colored stone,
waited until she rode off on her bicycle. Even with no one there
we hesitated going in, and didn't stay. Photographs looked at us
from tombstones. I liked the faces of the strange dead
on their graves, faces of men and women the rain washes into,
the real flowers. I liked the church doors open, the candles
          blooming.

In Blumenstein there's a marker cut with emblems: a scythe
leaning against a tree, a farmer's hat carved, his coat
folded over a hayrick. The work of a man's life is his language
and having heard, we were satisfied to know him by that dark
          stone,
his place in the earth. Herdsmen were home from the high
          pasture,
cows crowded the lane, the bells on their necks ringing praise
in a concert of joy melodious and clear between the mountains.

July Morning, Salzburg

Walking the *Glan*, I can't take my eyes
off the mountain: *die Untersberg*
regal with snow. In the lower meadows,
dandelions. Townfolk go by, strangers,
a handsome man with his dog. We exchange
smiles, he wants to talk and I
have no German. For this he is sorry
and he claims a common language
in the air and light around us,
water-music. Opening his arms
to everything, he says *Wunderbar!*
Word I know, my heart cries *Yes* to.

Fish Market

At the Marseilles fish market, a marvel of crustaceans,
spreading humps of gelatinous pink octopi, dark red
tuna steaks cut to the sound of bloody saws, the fishwife
callers shouting *bouillabaisse*, above the tubs and trays
the faces of men and women you could turn to and live with:
one sunburned laughing fisherman who held a big lobster
close to your face, clicked its claws open and shut
while years fell over backward until you believed yes, it's possible
you could love a man again, you could fish the Mediterranean
where this morning on the shore you rolled up your slacks and
ran into the sea in honor of your seventy-third birthday
and your feet turned cold while your heart went out
to the storied gods and goddesses, the lost enchanted islands.

Flight Pattern

Take nothing for granted, not this flight, this day
of departure, not your seat by the window, the man next to you
reading the shopper's catalogue, his heavy metal box
stowed in the overhead bin. The door could spring open.
Retrieving the box, he could drop it. Death is
riding one wing and beauty the other, each flawed event
with its peculiar seed of perfection, like my hope
that the woman on her way to Hong Kong found the right gate,
and on time. Take nothing for granted, not the ordinary
abstracted gaze of passengers crowding the aisle, not
rainbow puddles on the runway. The safety card
carries minimal information, and it is not certain
when this plane will take off or arrive. Each breath
is a chance you take, and more often than not
after the fumes burn clear, the air will be all right.
The pilot knows the route, and I could have told you
we may have to wait for our turn to climb into the sky,
but this plane will rise and our lives fly off into
and above the startling cover of cloud. Hours later
we will come down, some of us into the arms of people
who love us. In the journeys of the heart, be alert
for the slightest sign. Along the extraordinary blue
corridors of the soul, take nothing for granted.

With Friends in Hanazono

Dark comes to all the forty-nine temples
of Myoshinji. A parade of umbrellas in the rain,
we take seats in a courtyard, tell each other
it may be impossible to say what God sounds like,
and the rain means nothing except itself.
We give full attention to its many sounds
on wood and stone, bamboo, metal, the tile roofs,
on the hands and faces of our bodies which are not—
O could we believe it!—the enemy.

I think of the last time I allowed myself time
to listen to anything, how everything flows backward
and vanishes. Unsteady, drunk, weaving from side to side
on the wet stones, a monk wanders past. My friend says
he is escaping his holy life. Her apologetic laugh
accepts such need in these bodies we have borrowed.
Not perfect, we are good enough to listen, simply,
to rain from heaven, hoping perhaps, we may hear
what it is we are for.

Children in a Cemetery, Kyoto

mountain gate, a bucket
sandalwood dipper

Junko rinses her hands, pours water
to purify the ancestral marker

in July sun we name our lost
children; *Aioi*, hollyhock

her daughter who lived one hour
Philip, my stillborn son

in Japan Junko says if the child
is born alive, a name must be given

the death anniversary honored
it took years to name the boy

I never saw   here everyone who dies
is blessed by a new name

and Junko's grandmother left her life
as *Happy Child*   our children

almost visible, disturb nothing,
go from us in the sound of temple bells

At the Cedar Gate

On another birthday after my death, who will
open my books and listen to my heart, that unknown stranger
I want so much to hear? Already this singular moment
is turning its back and the past walks toward me
filled with surprises I could not accept. If I could I would not
go back. I am only looking for signs on a way that never repeats.

Shakuhachi music rises in the garden,
the monk who is playing stands in his shyness
behind the cedar gate. Bending to the wood, I breathe.
New bamboo tosses green in the sun. Young iris
grows in a river of stones.   This windy day
has nothing to do with my tears, they are
a gift of presence around me, your absence
on a path with strangers.

This is not a place of decision.
Even where four ways meet, the primary directions
are roots and the sky.   Wait.
There is nothing to decide. What is mysterious
is already under way: preparations for the feast,
connections in the atmosphere,
voices on invisible lines.

What I thought I wanted I thought I chose.
Today the shapes gather like clouds at the markers,
unacknowledged dancers in circles I moved in and out of
dreaming I was the center.   Always the monk
was ahead of me, playing his flute in that first garden
of spring snow when my newborn body met air
and the doctor ordered fire.

Who am I now to ask readers for words
that run in a stone river, gone
in the last clear notes of the *shakuhachi*,
the swaying bamboo, the fragrance of cedar?

She Who Travels Alone

No, not in Bristol or in Galway will I find him,
not Minneapolis or Sioux City. Though I am brave
and go as far as Antarctica, he does not
ride the ice floes or swim under frozen water.
He does not live with sheep in the Midlands
or walk the abandoned cloister. He
is not to be found on the benches in pubs
or the next seat at the theater. His shadow
does not hang on a thornbush or darken
the lost emerald lake in British Columbia.
The greenest of fields in Africa will not revive him,
or castanets in cantinas south of the border. He
does not rake stones in the Japanese garden,
sit silent and patient with open eyes in the zendo.
He does not lift luggage into the car or insist
on the open window. Though I am a tireless traveler
I cannot search out his face or bring him to bed.
The last kiss was *goodbye, God be with you*
most trusting and hopeful of prayers
for each restless departure,
each solitary coming home.

Passing Through

Easy enough
to collect postcards,
comment on the scenery,

watch petals fall and not
feel their weight, not breathe
with the breathing hills
or listen to sounds
that circulate the light.

Easy to say our interior sun
blazes with intense noon and then
not go where it's warm.

What calls me back
are times I wrote nothing down,
left the observation deck,
the highway viewpoint
and climbed the lavaflow
to the volcano,

ran the breathless incline
of sand and dunegrass
over broken shell
into the pounding, bittersalt Pacific.

Walking on the Beach

Driftwood, stones, the detritus
we collect from the shifting shores
and bring inland, we save for a while
on some shelf or window-ledge,
then give back to the beach
for others who gather such things.

Required as we are to live
with mystery as our only certainty
we pick up skeletons and shells
under the light of a Full Flower Moon,
and we go out each morning
pensive from our misunderstood dreams
into the holy tension of a day
that waits to inform us.

All that we gather and hold
we let go as we learn to be
and be content, keeping track
of the tides, the barometer,
alert to the slightest change of weather.

Two

A Habit of Conversation

The souls I love, a tireless tribe,
fall out of my life like seed. We can never
be done with each other.

On this side of the boundary
I sleep and wake up next to,
often in the morning of some long-past day,
how much, how little it matters
that the orange poppies loosen and drop
to the table, that twilight
is lonely with last sun on the houses,
the grass shifting into shadow
where children with nothing to protect or defend
play at final games before sleep.

Though we have no more need of each other,
our exaggerated important beliefs,
long habit of conversation persists,
gives speech and hearing to the dead
whose need I can't assess.

They didn't make it back.
I didn't think they would.

Light goes from every object in the room
and each stays here, in place, as we
in dark or day, keep ours,
we who rely on the usual words
and cannot be done.

For My Father

Where do you ride on the great dark horses
father of mine, in all your sleeping?
Where do they take you, the swift wild ponies
leaving us here in our wondering weeping?

Away from hurting and far from pain,
to the greenswept countryside again
where lovely music rises and fills
the hidden valleys, the Irish dells.

Where do the long roads carry you,
traveling father, across the land?
Where is the home for a wanderer
with the baggage of hope in his hand?

Light carves a road through the darkness
and the miles are a steady hum,
a luring charm of will-o-the-wisp
where the greener fields cry "Come!"

Where are the waters bearing you,
sea-loving father in all your dreaming?
Where do you wander watching the waves
rise and break with their secret meaning?

Far off to the lands of years ago
the oceans pull with their thunder song.
My heart goes out on the crests and swells
back to the time of nothing wrong.

Where do you go when we cannot follow
on the horses, the roads and the sea?
Where are you moving away from us
in the shadows of time and eternity?

    Back where the lords of laughter live
    in stories that never grow old,
    home to the generous heart of things
    to warm my heart that is tired and cold.

Last Words

If they talk to us, if they can, the dying
say words we turn into icons, rosary beads
we tell over and over, drawn to death as a subject
we have to be interested in. Sylvia Plath said
some have it, this talent for dying. Some don't.
We make metaphors, images, as if pictures
could help, hide the fact in phrases: biting the big radish,
shall we gather at the river, the last round-up,
crossing over, passing (though we don't know where).

Euphemisms for what is and will forever be,
mystery: pushing up the daisies, going home, snuffed out,
rubbed out, done in, going over the hill, drinking the stirrup cup
for one last ride. We expire, kick the bucket, go out feet first
or with our boots on, hoping to be ready for the big one,
the final game of cards, whatever hand the dealer gives us.

Stories help: Falstaff babbling of green fields,
Goethe calling for "Light! More light!"
Keats encouraging Severn, "Now you must be firm,
for it will not last long" and then at the last,
"Open the curtains, I don't want to go home in the dark."
The boy Sean tells his mother, "Truth is dark, but when you sing
I hear it," and George Fox, "At last I am clear, I am fully clear."

A heart specialist insists, no tubes for him: "You're not going to
make an idiot out of me." And the woman who loved flowers
tells her daughter to take them away, they pull oxygen out of the air,
more color than she can stand. A song, *"The bear went over*
the mountain to see what he could see." A cup of warm milk
and one word: "Peace." "I think I'm ready, but I don't want it
to take too long." Emily Dickinson's "flood subject"
before she was carried up the hill with lilacs,
"Called Back" carved into her stone.

The dying Tolstoy wrote on his bedsheets, work he wanted
to finish. And the young woman Michelle climbed into bed
beside her ninety-year-old friend with whom she'd sung duets,
sang the first verse of "I love you truly," answered only
by humming deep in the throat, words gone.

Last sounds like our first cries, incoherences, tears,
forlorn memories, stumblings where the living can't reach:
I'm so tired. So sorry. I can't do anything I want.
Water, please, I'm dry. Stop! Home! Mama! Goodbye!
I love you. Is it time for the news? Is Dan Rather on yet?
Don't hold me back! Now you have to see through my eyes.
Your face looks funny, are you ok? It hurts so much.
Forgive me. Rosebud! O Pacific!

*

In the Ring of Fire, the thirteen thousand islands east of Krakatoa,
children play in the caves of the dead, rearrange
the bones, dismantle skeletons, pile up the skulls. Fingers
probe eye sockets, leg bones useful in invented games.
Dying completes the cycle, cause for festivity, the roofs
of buildings curve up like smiles that say we
slide down into life and stay for awhile,
go back in the same motion,
our mouths turned toward happiness.

And what words from us as the dying go?
Leaning over, holding on, what do we breathe
into the unhearing ear? If the soul lingers and waits
listening, is there anything to say?
Where do words come from? How do we find them?

After my mother's stubborn, long leaving,
bending close to her head on the pillow,
I noticed how white, how fine her hair was,
lifted strands from one ear, whispered
without thought a hopeful phrase out of nowhere:
Happy landing!

Mother

If you could come up the walk
to the door of my house, if you could
rise in your favorite yellow suit and come
from your grave, find the silver archer
still pinned to the scarf at your throat
and have your legs work again so you
can walk the miles it would take
to get here to my time of living alone,
what would we find in common?

Over tea and *Scrabble*, the crossword puzzles,
poems you said and I say aloud in the empty room,
the lists you made and I make to remember
what's essential, to assert that this day
something waits to be accomplished, we might
give up controversy, be tender and steadfast,
make room for sorting between the layers,
these late learnings without which we die inside,
go to our graves heavy with the weight
of argument and difference. My slower steps
would walk unsteady beside you, my changing eyes
begin to see what I missed.

If you come, will you tell me how to improve my life,
insist I wear a scarf in this colder weather,
suggest I get a cat for company? Mothering dies hard
as you did, and as I may. What we could do
we did, loved each other. On this November day
of your birth and your death, in my diminished
and reminding house, I clap my hands for delight
in us, go to the door to welcome and let you in,
my sister, my friend.

Of Seven, This One

I do not envy the strong bright young
their hot and heedless blood,
the tangled sheets and sweet long nights.
We had ours while we could.

I would not ask them to forswear
if they could let such fealty go,
or stop my heart from praising them
so caught by heaven now.

But when I hear old lovers talk
or see them hand in hand
where laughter's low and private
and quick glances understand,

it's then that envy casts me down
in rage for all we will not have:
consummation of our years
the flat refusal of the grave.

Aspen

When the technician called your name, you went with him, left me
looking at the pictured wall of aspen grove, clones of trees
enlarging the MRI waiting-room to bring the outside in,
the inside out, my interior landscape of mountain green and gold:
long October drives in the Rockies, the expansive view
at the crest of the road before you go down.

On the Colorado plateau the trees blaze in hopeful light,
in Squaw Valley and in Utah the leaves shiver into music.
As words pretend to, and then refuse significant connection:
Aspen, a common species widely distributed
is easily cut and scarred. Sucker stems
feed off a central root system,
the ramets push toward sun that feeds them.
As if like aspen we could replicate
into theoretical immortality, live for a million years.

Our balance, too, is precarious, we wobble from test to test,
your *glioblastoma* destructive as fire or avalanche
that forces aspen seeds out of their holding pattern,
pushes the stems to harvest sunlight.

I turn to the trees as if your disappearance
into the scanning room
could mean you've gone instead
into the space of this photograph
that covers the entire wall.

Permission

Because this morning my neighbor's hundred-year-old dogwood
looks holy, a white-on-green mass, celebratory and solemn
as cathedral-going, because so many bluebells
swing in a small wind and I cut lilacs in slow rain,
enough to fill vases in rooms of this house you haven't seen
and won't, because it is the first of May fourteen years after,
I give myself permission to begin:

*

Wakened before first light, I hurried down the stairs,
found the night nurse closing your eyes,
presumptuous woman. Against your chest, I
cried what tears would come. In rage so mixed
with joy I couldn't say which mattered most,
pulled from your throat the tube endured for weeks.
Its end was brown as rust.

I helped the woman wash your body,
dressed you in worn familiar clothes,
knew exactly what you'd wear, nothing fancy,
nothing good or useful to be burned:

in blue denim shirt-pocket, dark and spikey rosemary
and in your stiffening fingers
dandelion, alyssum, daisy, forget-me-not,
common flowers from the yard.
Beside your head
a lighted candle.

Then all was done,
the living room transformed
as you
into a place, august, serene
as any empty tomb.

And with us in the room
a presence clear and clean. Call it
release or mystery,
the change.

Attentive

Sometimes the dead
who are alien and defiant
go on talking and singing
as if to test the range
of their new frequencies in the air

intermittent, past words and noise
the humming vibrations
escape the compressed layers
of time and death: stalactites' steady drip
in caves, voices out of steam and groan,
a hiss of lava flow, the rush behind
a waterfall's transparent curtain

tenuous neglected sounds
at the edges of quiet that is almost
but not quite, silence: insects making trails
in the dirt, wings opening and closing,
barely audible human sighs

I listen to each bud
that is ready to open,
put my ear
next to ice, melting

If I could I would tell you
how for love's sake
I am learning to be attentive
to all that is other,
and apart.

Whistle

a broken skate, my foot
drags down the black slide of water,
my body straining toward home,
that star-nest
a bright blur

the noise in my throat
could be music
on its way to a whistle

when did I
learn to do that,
when did I forget

and who runs to teach me
praise through pursed lips,

breaks the morning of my heart,
calls me to carry dark in my teeth
across the bitter water?

Northwest Woodcarver

The accident on the icy road cannot be undone,
the thieving black bird will not give up your daughter.
Careful with the sun he carries in his beak, he

tells his plans to no one. Who can say where he goes
with that incandescence, the light of your days?
In the dark that is quiet around me, the fire

makes shadows, fragrance curling off the cedar,
dust and chips at my feet. There is good conversation
between the gouge and the adz, the mallet.

From the block on my knees, the bird
will not be hurried. In the sorrow of my hands
the details: wing feathers and eyes,

the clawed feet, my work rough as a cry
from the raven, grief talking the limits
of life and memory, how far love goes.

The Hawk

Christmas afternoon. A neighbor said he'd seen
a red-tail early that morning, said the bird came in
fast and low, the telephone wire rocking and sagging
under the weight. Said it stayed a long time.

"It must've been my Dad." Words so quick
I don't know what called them into the air.

He was the first to see hawks, always, their rising
on thermals above the valley. I used to think he
brought them into range, the raptors suddenly there
and his eyes following as if he wanted to let go
and go with them. We couldn't get close to hawks.

Four years, and we're still measuring
the velocity of his going, the cancer
a chance hurricane that whirled him away.

If he could come back, maybe he would
come like this, so changed, so unannounced,
above our house that fierce gliding grace
and the folded heavy wings, the wild bird's
binocular vision, its splendid amazing eyes.

The Accident

Stumbling over ice in the field, the horse
pitches you under his belly, huge body
bearing down, hide steaming, each hair distinct,
big muscles working as he tries to find his balance
on the frozen dirt. And you on the ground,
under him. When finally he's off, the cold air
open at last between you, emptiness heavy
on your pelvis, you try to stand, and can't.
When you tell your leg to move, it doesn't.

The horse goes, comes back to look down at you.
Bigger than you remember, his wide nostrils
blow warm air in your face, his teeth yellow
in his mouth. Trying to get up any way you can,
you don't know why summer is all you remember:
riding the palomino bareback into the stable,
hay bales stacked clear to the roof, good leather smells
strong in the hanging harness and saddles. Newborn colts
on the straw. Twins. Good luck. So rare. And you
pick up the one with the joint ill, take him outside
into the sun, a world he might not live in. You feed him
by hand, he can't stand on his feet to nurse
and the other horses would kill him if they could.
You remember his perfect head, how he wanted
to stand, how he tried his legs and they wouldn't.
You called the vet, the rendering truck, never
talked about giving up, having to let him die.

A siren. Somewhere down the road, a siren.
The red lights turn in at your driveway. Snow
is coming at you, the wind rising hard and fast.
So many horses run alongside, their breathing
wet and white on the ambulance window.

for Pincy

All the Way Out

Visitors mean well, dutiful friends come by
but his room feels small. Flipping the pages
of familiar magazines, he hunts absent names.
Even his books are failing, his eyes. No language
he recognizes. Or those strangers who turn the TV too loud,
eat without talking, spill their food. He takes his meals
in his room, but nothing tastes right. The caretaker says
he can't stay, says she can't have him wandering off the way he does.
If he could, he'd say the poem. He's sure she's never heard of Yeats,
a song he hears in his head, over and over that music in his head:

> An agéd man is but a paltry thing,
> a tattered coat upon a stick....

That's it, that's where his Irish tweed jacket's gone
and the jaunty checkered hat with the feather in the band.
Hung on a stick somewhere. Not in his room. And he can't
find his wallet, his keys. He knew it was late afternoon
by the slant angle of sun in his eyes. Like the house-lights
going dim in the old Hartman Theater before the curtain went up
on the plays he loved, taking him out of himself.

He's surprised the poem comes back, he's forgotten so much:

> ...unless
> Soul clap its hands and sing...

Of course. *Unless* is what bothers him. No way
for his soul. No clapping hands. No singing.

Walking backward he was, into time, oceans
he'd crossed, Greek islands he'd sailed around,
rocky coastlines, lake country. So many rivers
and all of them coming together in this long stream
of light. Jesus walked on water, hoisted Peter
into that boat when faith failed. Well, his faith
wasn't going to fail, he had business to tend to,
someone coming toward him he wanted to meet,
hold onto, go away with. Once he'd been a praying man.
Any prayer he'd make now would be for less,
to speed the end. He knew what he wanted.
Even with the glare in his eyes he could walk.
Downhill. Straight to the water, and all the way out.

His body knew where he was going
on his way where light pulled him,
legs cutting the air,
the sandgrains
sifting into his shoes.

They Who Say Nothing

their job is to
go
away
and not come back
even when we ask them
Robert Bly, "Mourning Pablo Neruda"

We have this anxiety: if we don't think about them
the dead really will go away. If we forget
they'll leave us, and for good.
It will be our fault.

So we believe they want us to talk about them,
want our quickening thoughts, good or bad,
seldom or often: like leftover hardware
in the basement, cans of paint, scrap lumber
saved as Dad saved everything. And jokes:
like his using the wrong-size nails
to build the sunporch, the redwood siding
buckling under years of weather.

A friend doing it over, doing it right
asked Mom if she ever cussed out
her dear departed husband. "Oh, yes,"
she said, "many times."

Do they need us to keep them
close as neighbors next door,
do they want us telling
anecdotes and stories, are they
listening to what we say, can they
catch kisses in the air?

We want to help them, and we try
but finally we are faithless
as they are, they who say nothing,
turn from us and go.

In the Desert at Night

now that thoughts of cool prevail
how important it is that the tongue

give way to the heart and the new moon
keep its shadow

now I am separated from my kind
and entering a difficult language

can you understand
what I say, you are so quiet

on the road to light
what do my bones know

in the desert where is the touch
that defines and empties

now we are estranged and I cannot
take your hand

now that your hand does not exist
how important the tongue, the moon.

Three

Stones in a New Landscape

*You put two things together to make something
else...the better the fit...the greater the pleasure
from the making.*
John Jerome, *Stonework*

Riverstones hand-picked from Tenino Quarry, each
washed for years by water and grit, smoothed and pocked
and veined, a residue of plants and creatures in the crevices,
the small holes. Stacked in the truck-bed with its hydraulic
levers, chains, the hoist, the load is carried to my house,
set out on the sidewalk where the builder eyeballs the lot,
chooses among them, turns the stones one by one
in his hands, sets the trouble-fits aside.

On his knees, without gloves, he hears through his fingers
what a stone has to say, where it wants to go.
Such mindless ability to listen, he says is what teaches you.
If you keep at it more than six hours he says your brain
goes numb, the wall loses rhythm, the flow stops.
Base stones lined up against the slope are pushed well
into soil, a mix of sand and clay. Tamping the dirt
between layers, he adjusts flats and rounds, their weight,

fits edges and curves together. I think of Robert Frost
mending the line with his neighbor, how I love this wall
that keeps nobody in or out, the mottled white and gray
and brown at rest and touching, the builder's singular
body of work holding my house at its center, patterns
that settle and anchor the corner. If I learn to be quiet
there could be conversation with the green basalt of my
walk, stones in the wall, weeds that will root between them.

Visiting in Amherst: Two Poems

1.

It is a busy Summer—
I can't go to her grave,
Can't make the pilgrimage
So many others have—

I'm tendered when I hear of things
The constant pilgrims leave—
Their coins and candles, paper scraps,
a fan she will not wave—

Messages I'd like to give
to Emily, buried here
With lilac boughs and greenery
and poems in the air—

I say instead to Amherst hills,
her words upon the wind—
If she's with Carlo she may catch them—
My love without a sign.

2.

Summer is rich in fields and flowers,
the insects and birds so generous,

the lovely indifferent plants
with their flourishing signatures.

Outside and within, behind each day's
surfeit of joy, a question: what if

there really is a God alive and at work
in the lush thickness of things,

in the disappearing edges of green
and gold-blue air? What if nothing

is strange, not even the question,
and the universe is a body like my own,

disheveled and rich in the cycle
of seasons? This morning in Amherst

at the turn of the river, before my eye
makes it around a curve, I almost see

the gambrels bracing the roof—
Emily's house, a fair Possibility.

Tulips

1. Primary Shape

Miss Fenton hands out the paper,
red, yellow, green. Blunt scissors
on the low table, a jar of library paste,
the stubby, black-bristled brush
with a bent tin handle.

The tulip is a primary shape, she says,
a cup. She says to cut three ovals, arrange them
on the stem. Add two leaves, and paste.
The paste smells and tastes like spearmint.
Dries fast, crusts your fingers.
The brush thickens.

2. The Bulbs

Last winter's gift from Anne, who said they
were all purple, but they came up salmon pink,
scarlet, gold. A parade of upright, solitary
flowers. Not for cutting. Not lasting.
Fading, like the tulips on the bedsheets
where she falls asleep dreaming of seed catalogues,
baskets of fat brown bulbs that will open next spring
into Heart's Delight, Princess Irene, Yellow Dawn,
the Queen of the Night. She walks through
fringed and ruffled and striated,
the first and last, the double and single,
early and late.

3. Fields in the Skagit Valley

To catch this immaculate joy, be where there is
no *was*, where the eye so used to green can't stop
moving from one bright field to the next, more
to take in than heart and eye can, acres of color
splashed down in layers clear to the horizon, bold
as a Van Gogh painting under a gray sky.

Look where a child runs between the rows!
Her parents call to her, they want to take pictures
but she keeps running. O there are more and more
and so many she can't stop where there's no end to tulips,
thousands in a sea around her, this ocean of red and purple,
these pink and yellow waves.

There is nothing but flamed orange and dark apricot,
edged plum and vermilion, carmine and currant red,
scarlet satin, and the soft rose violet fading to
white coral. All the way as far as she can see
and she runs, hair flying behind her, her feet
lifting and falling on the rich clumped earth.
She wants to hold them, the colors, and she races
toward each and all, lost in the tulip fields,
gone quite out of reach and time, into glory.

Blackberry-Picking

for Galway Kinnell

One blackberry poem our limit, the poet said
who'd already written his, as if to say
there's only one such possible epiphany,
say the blackberries won't keep their black shine
always, or even for so long as we've energy
to pick them. This morning the red-dark juice
lusts into purple, stains my fingernails,
covers the moons and cuticle, bloody scratches
show on my wrists and hands, there are snags
in my jeans, and berries in the freezer, this poem
one of many I may write before the season ends.
There are lots of ways to say *blackberry-picking*,
harvest that goes on and on, ripening in so many
patches alongside so many roads. The over-ripe
fall through my fingers, lost between the bush
and the basket, the best and blackest
shine through the sharpest thorns
and just out of reach
drawing me into the thicket.

On Studying Whitman Indoors

Come into this classroom, Walt.
Turn us all out of doors. Take us
to the long beaches to read your poems.
Shout your words against the breakers,
the cry of gulls and the sea's wind.
Fling your arms about us
where we sit huddled over your books,
timid, in glasses.
Teach us new laughter, lust.
Point us toward miracles.
Show us our city and the open road.

Barefoot in the grass,
stretched out, breathing hard
and touching one another,
we could believe you.
We are your children and comrades.
We know how to walk in this or any weather.

In the Open

Cornfields in late fall,
the last summer heat
rising off clumps of dirt,
dry leaves and the stalks
clicking, clear air
flowing like a rush of water,
and two boys galloping
up and down the long rows
in and out of stubble
slapping their hands and whinnying
Let's be horses! Let's be horses!

Sea Song Out of *Beowulf*

Dree me to nim the swan-road, breast-hoard, suffer me
to hold the sea's storehouse, thole and take hold
of the bone-house, body-box, dree the skeleton store,
all the way suffer and endure the body walking light on the sea,
the body walking and the swan-road a-sheen, the body's trunk
walking on the sea shining. Thole the breast-hoard,
nim the bone-house, seize the body-box, suffer
the store of thoughts and feelings home to the sea,
dree the skeleton all the way to the sea, the swan-road a-sheen
in the morning, the sea shining and singing in the morning.

Eelgrass, Padilla Bay

One of the richest places on earth, and for now to have only
one teaching: examine the eelgrass, how it moves in these
deceptive green meadows that reach all the way to open water,
how the thick roots might teach me to stabilize the muddy bottom
of my life, give shelter to any small attaching animals, offer
nutrient source for whatever remains as the tides come in and go out.

Content to forego instructions that tell me how to walk on the
        mudflats
where a heel-toe rhythm breaks the suction, I sit in the beach-wrack
and start to sketch one particular hag of a tree festooned with
ribbons of eelgrass, try to catch the feel only of this, notice how
the streamers lie combed all one way over the branches, in the crotch
and the notches, how the grasses bend and sway in the light wind.

I pull a strand from a large pile, stretch it between my fingers,
this tough fibrous green that could go for a basket, a mattress.
Lifting and separating the pieces, I make a nest that is wet and cool,
almost ready to take me down where animals I do not know could be
waiting. They didn't invite me here, and I am slow to learn the rules
of their hospitality. The beach feels dangerous, pregnant
with possibility. I think of Millay's poem, "Ebb Tide":

these wet rocks where the tide has been
the bottom of the sea once more
no fit place for a child to play

Child who is here where the sea was, where the brackish water
turns itself over and around and went out and will come again
in another turning of stones and driftwood, shells, I sit with my back
against a tangled mass of eelgrass, consider the eelgrass, *Zostera
            marina,*
the little I have learned about it, how I can't get close enough
to learn from it. Gulls cry around and above me, crows. In the
            distance
the hills and islands reverse themselves in the water, upside-down.
I like looking at these dark images that float and break and are
suspended. Out on the gooshy meadows in the fecund life of this
            estuary
where salt and fresh waters meet, the raucous birds cry their own
            music.
There will always be more. The eelgrass flowers under water and
            decays
in the tides that are both takers and givers, and the fine sea air
moving in and out of my lungs delivers and receives messages.

Claiming the Season

after D.H. Lawrence

Not every man has gentians in his house.
Nor every woman, either. This terrible autumn
gold will have to do, and it does: gold light
gathering the earth to rest, the grasses turning
and returning, gold that is, and is burnished,
burnishing bronze light warming to the touch,
sun I pull into my body, that my body welcomes,
fire enough to give beauty back, gold enough
to linger on the snow, gold edges in the sky,
gold leaking into gray pewter, into the small corners.
Not every woman has gentians in her house
or chooses blue for going into the dark. I claim
gold, falling on and into the hills, harvest
in the trees, filtered bright gold taking the leaves
and letting them go, this gold going easiest of all.
Reach me goldenrod, hand me gold roses and rich
yellow flowers. Let them burn and die back.
Give me gold stubble in the field, bright pumpkins.
Gold to go with me descending, and not to be
exchanged or traded for any other light.

Peripheral Vision

You taught me this: a sideways turning, a star
reappearing in another space when I shift my sight,

the slant light, peripheral vision for what moves alongside
real and elusive as the edges of seasons that almost

escape us and turn into measures full and running over,
a surfeit of beauty at risk and just out of reach, everything

the eye takes in before it closes, the pictures we want to
hold onto completing themselves in the dark. Having looked

hard and far, tried to take in words and the full day,
our limited portion of heaven in the night sky, when we

come to where we are and can't say where we are except that
we go on walking through such time as we have, may there be

light at the margins. When the direction we think we're going
changes, may we in this early northern dark be aware of disturbance

at the corner of the eye. And see the young perfect deer
suddenly there, disappearing into the trees.

Island Ferry

Off the wet deck of the Nisqually Ferry
and looking into scumbled distance,
I think of ancient Chinese scrolls, paintings
with low hills and dark islands rising
out of rain and mist, as the San Juans rise for us
moving down the channels past Brown Island
to Orcas and Lopez, Shaw. The gray and silver water
goes on and on, opening to coves and inlets, bays.
At the stern, the wake foams and churns, lightens
to pale green. Leaning against the railing, shifting
positions to meet the wind, I put my glasses
into my pocket, invite my eyes and skin
to take in this weather. Drenched and happy
without words or wants, I bow to the stranger
walking past me on the deck when she says
"This is better than meditation." We face into the wind
like the glaucous-winged gulls taking shelter
in protected space over and around the boat,
hitching rides on the deck-rail. Long-falling
the rain barely disturbs the water that takes it in
and smoothes over, ready for more. Blurred and foggy
my eyes try to see, a vision farther in. Holding
the Chinese masters in mind I remember wisdom
in paintings with small figures against mountains and waterfalls.
Acknowledging my own proportionate nature, chilled and wet,
I go inside to get warm and dry. But for minutes only.
Conversation is not what I want or need,
not when the islands are rising and falling away
and the rain will not blow against me like this, ever again.
Not for any poem I could write, any memory of sadness or art.

Four

Dogwood

Late Letter to an Early Love

Dear Jim

In this photograph the camera angle tilts you
taller than you were, big against the sky,
one hiking-booted foot on the downslope of the hill,
your smile as I remember.

I'm writing for the sake of a poem that eludes me.
A long time it's tried to make it, get free of rhyme
it's caught in, impossible green and gold. Forty years
and your dogwood's still fastened in my hair, my shoes
still tied to your belt as if we're still crossing that creek
in the Hocking Valley, the glitter of sun and water
between us, my young fantasies of love surprised
by the small miracle of *you* asking *me* to walk with you,
your hand on the long stretch up, the trail disappearing.

In California, Jim, I live close to the sea
where dogwood flowers in April on Bear Creek Trail
near Point Reyes. I came to see if one particular tree
lights the hills the way they say it does. In high grasses
mixed with mint and blue periwinkle I sit on a stone
and make notations, looking for the poem. An orange butterfly
is poised on the wild blackberry, an ant climbs my hand.

The flowers are as I remember: white and legendary,
crown-bearing blossoms with flat petals
rounding to rust-colored points. A squirrel drinks rainwater
where the moss-covered trunk and branches meet, a jay
surprises me with music. The music I listen for
doesn't come on a regular beat, my life's less guarded
than it was, a clearing where light comes down.
And water at the roots.

Like this great tree, my new poem invites animals, the rain, and butterflies. And Jim, I need to tell you, as beautiful as spring flowers, in the fall the dogwood drops red and purple leaves into the stream.

Picking Plums

The bucket's full. Smoke
rubs off the plums
I've picked by reaching up,
around, and through
the branches of this tree
beside the road.

Dull hazed blue and
yellow red, plum skins are
many. Some yield
to finger touch. The cracks show
juice. The firm ones
ripen in a day or two.

This tree was one
I watched. It leans.
The fruit helped balance things.
The leaves are nearly
gone. A few keep hold,
and stay.

My hands are stained.
They run with purple lines.
they smell ripe as the darkening air.
I go home rich, fragrant with
plums, warm as the tree,
in a different wind.

Night in August

Unmixed with consolation the moonless hours
go by. In their long passing and forfeit to sleep
I attend the burial of secrets, today's
accumulation of riddles. I had forgotten

such occasions outweigh the light, how far
outside the limits of the outer eye the inner
opens: on specters in doorways, *consonantia*
of wind and crickets, the summer earth

heavy with heat. What changes is the felt density
of things: the singular freight of the empty bed,
boxes on the dresser more surely there in the dark,
each shapeless object defined by its presence

in the unlighted room. Ceremony that goes on
as the body relinquishes attention and the day
delivers itself to clouds unveiling the moon
high and white on the peerless shores of sleep.

October Moon, New England Church

The full moon's reflected light
blesses the fallen and blazing
sacrament of leaves on the ground,
beech and oak the last to go,
into thin glacial soil where life
lives on granite. The creatures
are preparing, hoarding
what they will need.

Fatten yourself like the moon
and get ready for sleep, then
while the earth freezes around you
move in your house like a tunnel,
stretch your full length of muscle and sinew,
your blood warmer than the snake's
who may not make it.

When you are called to come out into spring
perhaps then will be the time to live,
when hunger has taught you to be thin
as a spire narrowing into heaven,

If you sleep far enough and long
your eyes returning from the dark
to the waking green of the world
will be luminous with gifts,
each astonishment you thought lost
you take with you, into the sun.

Calling the Barred Owl

If the owls are here
they do not answer
or fly to us. Even if they are
in the trees and look down
through the branches and leaves,
they are unfooled by imitation calls
and do not reply.

Stumbling in the woods
out past our usual bedtime
and eager to belong in the dark world,
we want the owls
to trade signals,
acknowledge our mutual calling
back and forth at night.

For the Good Luck Child with Golden Hair and the Snowstars Melting

I watched her, she flew on her skates
turning circles on the frozen pond, her blades
spit splinters of ice, she was wild, she was dancing
and her arms in the sleeves of her sweater made wings
in the air where she bent low and gliding
on one leg like a tall winter bird. O she was sweet,
she was lovely and her hair caught the wind
that brought roses and left them there in her cheeks,
left sapphires in her vivid eyes. O she was green
and gold on the shaved white ice, oblivious
to charms, and we in her blessing
took everything she gave to us.

for Francesca, her 13th birthday

January Moss

On this side of the year
when the sun drifts off and we go inside
and don't know what we're looking for
as we wait for light and watch it
passing, if a sign could find us,
a stab of wonder, the tinkering would end,
the puzzling disguises.

Whatever comes
comes out of the tangle,
out of this bent and bending
time, these precise moments
our lives are made of.

For all we know
if we wait, if we can,
the nexus will hold us,
the roots consenting to change
fragile and enduring
as moss underfoot
greening in the wet season
another cycle of weather.

The Seals

Silver sheen on dark rocks
tells me that the seals
have hauled themselves
into the sun, large eyes
closed against such dreams
as they may have: walrus

knocking pups off the ice floes,
long yellow tusks
slashing soft bellies,
sucking out the organs,
peeling the bodies he shakes
back and forth, swallowing
what's left; hunters with clubs
and after the skinning, blood
melting into the snow.

In my own nightmares
I have such fear
for our vulnerable children,
want the killing stopped,
want impossibly the walrus
and men not to be what we are,
want the seals to keep their eyes open.

Against What Comes

How without weariness water
makes openings through leaves and debris,
logs. This March afternoon the sun
melts ice on the hill where all morning
children careened and bumped on cardboard sleds.
Even at risk to my bones I wanted to slide
and did not. By five o'clock the ice
hardens, turns blue. Thawing and freezing
go on, like suffering, like the real thing.

Here's no room for pain conjured
from the hurt of others. Too much news
from too many places and my apocalyptic dread
mushrooms. It's not hard to pretend
to suffer so, a waste. Courage must be
practiced against what comes. Here, now
the shoots of lichen, *tilandesia*, like wiry
little bushes spring out of cracks. When I
push the green wires in, they jump back
toward the sun.

Last year's curled-up leaves soften, shine.
The lodgepole pines that held the heavy
weight of snow are straighter, and chipmunks
are out. Persistent and turbulent, the water
fascinates. I let go the imagined bodies,
blood in other places, my easy sympathy,
try to make ready for the real anguish
waiting like rocks in the river.

If Death Is a Woman

she's not content with half-measures, takes what she wants
when she wants it. If she plays chameleon wife
or stepsister to power, it's because she's already won
and knows it. We can't get away from her, *dark mother*
always gliding near with soft feet. However we name her
she's ready to rock us through nightsweats into silence.
Nobody escapes. If death is a woman
she wants a clean house, she's beating prayer rugs
to get it, washing down the bloody streets,
dancing on all the open, hidden graves.

Listen, John Donne

The voice of tolling bells is everywhere.
I cannot answer all these dirges on the air.
Knell and tocsin summon me for miles around,
I walk each hour through heavy din of sound.
There's such a pulling tide of mournful woe
that if I would I could not send to know.
Which bell is mine upon the mourning air?
How know the sound for which I am to care?

Set deep within there's rhythm to the whole,
a certainty of answer in the soul.
One pulse is steady through the tolling tide.
Alone upon that heartbeat sound I ride.
Then let announcements and alarums come,
proclaim disaster on bell, on wind and drum.
The bell that tolls for me's a single sound.
I cannot answer for the country round.

All Dance One Dance

the wise man is a dancer
the fool wants to know all the steps first
Sam Keen

even if the end of a thread
is all we have to dance from
one foot follows the other

in motion and in stillness
the dance remembers us,
gives a body permission to fly

we can't see the pattern
our footsteps leave,
the configuration

cars make on the freeway,
the red and white lights
stopping   turning
pulling ahead

unless you push down
you can't leap into the air
meet the old crone gypsy woman
in a funky bar in Spain
dancing grief for a grandson

join Zorba on the beach

a deranged woman
jumping into the unfinished sand painting,
the Tibetan monks
returning without dismay to make another,
their whole and half circles
embracing the demonic, then
letting it go as they
carry the colored sand back to the sea

let the heart break every day
and perhaps you can dance Butoh

find the grand right and left
that lets you promenade home

even if the end of a thread
is all we have to dance from
one foot follows the other.

The Headlands

Tell us what you know. Before you go, tell us
how hard you tried to keep up, how you
came upon the white dog and knew you couldn't
take him home, how the afternoon under the rusty oaks
was only your longing to be somewhere else, wanting
the breakers below the headlands, the roar of the sea
crashing inland, carrying you to the cliffs
and you realize it's not you who is suffering
but another who looks just like you and dies there
with foam and salt on his lips, the red poppies in his hands.

Narrow Boat, Long River

O let us talk of quiet that we know
—D.H. Lawrence, "The Ship of Death"

In the canoe now, on a long bright river, she
watches his shoulder muscles flex and relax as he pulls,
dips the paddle and pulls again, pushing the water back.

If she could find her voice she'd shout at the faces
around her bed, their senseless muttering mouths.
If words would come to her dry throat, she'd say the sun
is warm on the green water, the circles opening, widening,
closing over. She'd rise from this bed and take them with her
into the circles where she's drowning, those faces
leaning over, looking down, waiting for her to die.

She's waiting to sing light over the straight young back
of her love in the bow of the narrow boat, sing
the way he keeps the rhythm steady, the canoe
sliding ahead into the sun rising in the water drops,
light that goes out when his paddle dips and falls.

In Heavy Fall of Rain

What fierce power breaks me down like days
of windblown rain hard-sweeping the ground?
The water comes and comes and bends the grasses
flat, pummels the land with slant and shining
fists. I am not reconciled to this, unable
in my drenched and swelling state to praise
the deluge, see behind the shifting sun
the green I most will grow from. Is even flood
well-meant that storms and strains the banks
and boils and takes and makes that stunning roar?
O age comes on me strange and wild as this
with crack and hiss, no easy sunlit pass
on stubbled harvest fields, but chaos, noise,
the never-letting-up of wind, the drowning rain.

Anniversary

The meadow is not far away
and the log I leaned against
watching first light on the Trinity River,
watersounds like your hands
moving over and under me in the meadow
that is not far away. The magic of return
would undo me, it would unravel sleep
to feel your weight in motion against me,
see the sweatstains under your arms,
hear your voice run aground on stones
in the river of flowers and grass,
the meadow that is not gone
and is not far away.

Wasp in the House

In mid-March the first insect
finds its way into the house.
The dog lets me know. That buzz
at the window signals something
wrong, and she wants my lap
as the wasp wants out. The trick
is waiting for the exact moment
to turn the drinking-glass into
a prison, slide the paper under
the rim, hold it there, and walk
to the door. The trick is patience,
dexterity. As when tired of words
and the world, I am able to befriend
some small humming complexity
and let it go.

Before Sleep I Go Outside

What is more beautiful than Orion and the stars
seen through the bare limbs of an oak?

What too is more beautiful than winter clouds in a rush
over the face of the moon, when the mind gives way

and the supple body slows, the heart grown ready
to make the experiment: to be lifted and stretched

by measureless new dimensions? All that I have said
and heard recedes, pulled into space where there are no

words, my head quiet and at rest, leaning back
against a corner of the garage, under this night sky

and the far stars where my thirsty eyes drink as from
a pitcher that pours and pours and does not empty.